FOREIGN POLICY ASSOCIATION

Headline Series

No. 263   MARCH/APRIL 1983 $3.00

VIETNAM
The War Nobody Won

by Stanley Karnow

From *Vietnam: A History* by Stanley Karnow, © 1983 by Stanley Karnow and WGBH Educational Foundation, to be published by The Viking Press as a companion to the WGBH television series, "Vietnam: A Television History," beginning October 4, 1983 on PBS.

The Author

Award-winning journalist STANLEY KARNOW's
latest book, *Vietnam: A History,* reflects over 30
years' experience. His firsthand observation of
Vietnam began in 1959 when he arrived in Hong
Kong as bureau chief for *Time* and *Life* magazines. He has served as correspondent for *The
Washington Post* and NBC News, columnist for
the Des Moines Register and Tribune Syndicate,
foreign editor of *The New Republic,* 1973–75,
and contributing editor to *Newsweek International.* A Harvard graduate, he was a Nieman Fellow
in 1958 and a fellow of Harvard's East Asia Research Institute in 1971. He is
currently visiting associate, Harvard University Center for European Studies.
His other books are *Southeast Asia* and *Mao and China: From Revolution to
Revolution.*

Photo by Catherine Karnow

The Foreign Policy Association

The Foreign Policy Association is a private, nonprofit, nonpartisan educational
organization. Its purpose is to stimulate wider interest and more effective
participation in, and greater understanding of, world affairs among American
citizens. Among its activities is the continuous publication, dating from 1935, of
the HEADLINE SERIES. The authors are responsible for factual accuracy and for
the views expressed. FPA itself takes no position on issues of United States
foreign policy.

9995698

The HEADLINE SERIES (ISSN 0017-8780) is published five times a year, January,
March, May, September and November by the Foreign Policy Association, Inc., 205
Lexington Ave., New York, N.Y. 10016. Chairman, Leonard H. Marks; President,
William E. Schaufele, Jr.; Editor, Nancy L. Hoepli; Associate Editor, Ann R. Monjo;
Assistant Editor, Mary E. Stavrou. Subscription rates, $12.00 for 5 issues; $20.00 for
10 issues; $28.00 for 15 issues. Single copy price $3.00. Discount 25% on 10 to 99
copies; 30% on 100 to 499; 35% on 500 to 999; 40% on 1,000 or more. Payment must
accompany order for $6 or less. Second-class postage paid at New York, N.Y.
POSTMASTER: Send address changes to the HEADLINE SERIES, Foreign Policy
Association 205 Lexington Ave., N.Y., N.Y., 10016. Copyright 1983 by Foreign
Policy Association, Inc. Composed and printed at Science Press, Ephrata, Pa.

Library of Congress Catalog No. 83-81891
ISBN 0-87124-083-1

Introduction

Yes, we defeated the United States. But now we are plagued by problems. We do not have enough to eat. We are a poor, underdeveloped nation. Waging a war is simple, but running a country is very difficult.

—Pham Van Dong

Vietnam is still with us. It has created doubts about American judgment, about American credibility, about American power— not only at home, but throughout the world. It has poisoned our domestic debate. So we paid an exorbitant price for the decisions that were made in good faith and for good purpose.

—Henry A. Kissinger

The memorial, an angle of polished black stone subtly submerged in a gentle slope, is an artistic abstraction. Yet its simplicity dramatizes a grim reality. The names of the dead engraved on the granite record more than lives lost in battle: they represent a sacrifice to a failed crusade, however noble or illusory its motives. In a larger sense they symbolize a faded hope—or perhaps the birth of a new awareness. They bear witness to the end of America's absolute confidence in its moral exclusivity, its military invincibility, its manifest destiny. They are the price, paid in blood and sorrow, for America's awakening to maturity, to the recognition of its limitations. With the young men who died in Vietnam died the dream of an "American century."

Thousands of Vietnam veterans streamed into Washington on a crisp November weekend in 1982, along with their families and the families of the dead, to dedicate the memorial. Some were paraplegics in wheelchairs, others amputees. They wore fatigues or business suits, and several came in full combat gear. There were speeches and reunions and a parade, and a solemn service at the National Cathedral, where volunteers had held a candlelight vigil throughout the week, reciting the names of the nearly 58,000 killed and missing in action, one by one. From afar, the crowds resembled the demonstrators who had stormed the capital during the Vietnam war to denounce the conflict. But past controversies were conspicuously absent this weekend. Now Americans appeared to be redeeming a debt to the men who had fought and died—saluting their contribution, expiating their suffering. The faces, the words of dedication, and the monument itself seemed to heal wounds. The two names at the head of the memorial—Dale R. Buis and Chester M. Ovnand—evoked my own recollection of a distant event.

I first visited South Vietnam in July 1959, soon after arriving in Asia as chief correspondent for *Time* and *Life* magazines. Insurgents were just emerging to challenge the regime created there five years before, when an international conference held in Geneva, Switzerland, had partitioned the country following the French defeat. The term Vietcong, a pejorative label invented by the South Vietnamese government to brand the rebels as Communists, had not yet been conceived—and they were still known as the Vietminh, the movement that had vanquished the French. Several hundred American military advisers had been assigned to train and equip the South Vietnamese army, but signs of serious trouble were rare. Then, on the evening of July 8, an incident occurred at a camp near Bienhoa, the headquarters of a South

Vietnamese army division 20 miles northeast of Saigon. I drove there the next day to gather the details.

Six years later, when the United States was pouring men, money, and matériel into an expanding struggle, Bienhoa became the site of a gigantic American base, and the town degenerated into a sleazy tenderloin of bars and brothels. In 1959, however, it was still a sleepy little provincial seat—its church, stucco villas, and tree-lined streets the remnants of a century of French colonial presence. Driving through the heat and humidity of a tropical morning, I caught my first glimpses of a land still undisturbed by war. Peasants in black pajamas and conic straw hats bent over rice stalks in flooded fields, the slow rhythm of their labor testimony to the infinite patience of Asia, and busy village markets along the route advertised the country's fertility. But pulling into the army camp, I could almost taste the start of a war whose eventual magnitude would have then strained my wildest fancies.

The night before, six of the eight American advisers stationed at Bienhoa had settled down in their mess after supper to watch a movie, *The Tattered Dress,* starring Jeanne Crain. One of them had switched on the lights to change a reel when it happened. Guerrillas poked their weapons through the windows and raked the room with automatic fire—instantly slaying Major Buis and Master Sergeant Ovnand, two South Vietnamese guards, and an eight-year-old Vietnamese boy.

The Americans were not the first U.S. soldiers killed in Vietnam. Lieutenant Colonel A. Peter Dewey of the Office of Strategic Services had been gunned down accidentally by a Vietminh band outside Saigon as far back as September 1945. And a daredevil American pilot, Captain James B. McGovern— nicknamed Earthquake McGoon after a character in the *Li'l Abner* comic strip—crashed to his death while flying supplies to the beleaguered French garrison at Dienbienphu in May 1954. But Buis and Ovnand were the first to die during the Vietnam Era, the official American euphemism for a war that was never formally declared.

My dispatch about the incident at Bienhoa earned only a modest amount of space in *Time* magazine—it deserved no more. For nobody could have imagined then that some 3 million Americans would serve in Vietnam—or that nearly 58,000 were to perish in its jungles and rice fields and their names to be etched, 23 years after, on a memorial located within sight of the monuments to Washington and Lincoln.

Nor did I then, surveying the bullet-pocked villa at Bienhoa, even remotely envision the holocaust that would devastate Vietnam during the subsequent 16 years of war. More than 4 million Vietnamese soldiers and civilians on both sides—roughly 10 percent of the entire population—were to be killed or wounded. Most of the South Vietnamese dead were interred in family plots. Traveling in the north of the country after the war, I observed neat rows of whitewashed slabs in every village cemetery, each bearing the inscription *Liet Si*, "Hero." But the tombs were empty; the bodies had been bulldozed into mass graves in the south, where they had fallen.

In human terms at least, the war in Vietnam was a war that nobody won—a struggle between victims. Its origins were complex, its lessons disputed, its legacy still to be assessed by future generations. But whether a valid venture or a misguided endeavor, it was a tragedy of epic dimensions.

1

The Roots of
American Intervention

History is an organic process, a continuity of related events, inexorable yet not inevitable. Leaders and the people who follow them make and support choices, but within the context of their experience and aspirations. The roots of the American intervention in Vietnam were planted and nurtured in what sociology professor Daniel Bell has called America's concept of its own "exceptionalism."

"Westward the course of empire," wrote George Berkeley, the Anglican bishop and philosopher, heralding fresh horizons ahead as he departed from England for America in 1726. And, a century later, other Europeans echoed his celebration of the new society. To German philosopher Hegel, America was "the land of the future," beckoning "all those who are weary" of the old Continent, while the French statesman and author Alexis de Tocqueville perceived it to be a beacon, its democratic institutions, natural wealth, and individual opportunities serving as a model for decadent Europe, torn by poverty, frustration, class tensions, and ideological turmoil. The notion of singularity also inspired Americans themselves, and the freighted phrase manifest destiny signified belief in their obligation to export their benefits to less privileged civilizations abroad.

The phrase, coined in 1845 to promote the annexation of Texas, was originally intended to justify America's expansion toward its natural boundaries. It was the slogan of reformers, the sponsors of the Homestead Act, who sought to open new territories to small farmers, among them the German and Irish immigrants who had fled to the young United States in quest of freedom and security. Soon it was amplified by such idealists as poet Walt Whitman, who foresaw America projecting its "happiness and liberty" to the ancient cultures of Asia. Later, progressives like Presidents John F. Kennedy and Lyndon B. Johnson, convinced they were extending their liberal ethic to Vietnam as an antidote to totalitarianism, might have borrowed from Whitman:

Facing west from California's shores,
Inquiring, tireless, seeking what is yet unfound,
I, a child, very old, over waves, towards the house of maternity,
    the land of migrations, look afar,
Look off the shores of my Western sea, the circle almost
    encircled. . . .

The doctrine of manifest destiny was distinct from the imperialist dynamic that flourished around the turn of the century. The United States did reach out to grab the Hawaiian islands, Guam, and part of Samoa, and it took over Puerto Rico, Cuba, and the Philippines after defeating Spain. But while the European powers were then carving up Asia and Africa, there was little inclination in America for dominating foreign territories. In contrast to the Europeans, who needed overseas raw materials and outlets for their industries, the United States could rely on its own resources and a vast domestic market. Besides, as former rebels against oppressive British colonialism, Americans were instinctively repelled by the idea of governing other peoples. Distinguished molders of opinion at the time, like industrialist and philanthropist Andrew Carnegie and President Charles W. Eliot of Harvard, vigorously opposed imperialism, asserting among their arguments that it violated free trade.

So Cuba was granted independence, and bids by Haiti and San Domingo to become American dominions were rejected. The United States, unlike the Europeans, refrained from plunging into the plunder of China—and characteristically used an indemnity fund for damages incurred during the Boxer uprising of 1900 to school Chinese in the United States. The Philippines, the major possession to remain under American tutelage, were finally subdued after a protracted "pacification" campaign which foreshadowed U.S. strategy in Vietnam. But even before that conquest was completed, the Philippines were scheduled for eventual autonomy. Their acquisition had scarcely been hailed with jingoistic fervor, as President William McKinley later confessed: "The truth is, I didn't want the Philippines, and when they came to us as a gift from the gods . . . there was nothing left for us to do but take them all and to educate the Filipinos . . . and, by God's grace, do the best we could do for them."

It would be a gross distortion to suggest that the U.S. presence abroad was consistently prompted by such benign altruism. Big business exploited "our little brown brothers" in the Philippines just as it manipulated the economies of Latin America, often underwriting local despots in order to defend its interests. But a more prevalent strain in American expansionism was evangelical—as if the United States, fulfilling some sacred responsibility, had been singled out by the divinity for the salvation of the planet. The rhetoric of redemption permeated President Woodrow Wilson's pledges to "make the world safe for democracy" under American auspices. President Franklin D. Roosevelt emphasized the same theme. He encouraged nationalistic self-determination in European colonial areas, while denying that the United States had any hegemonistic ambitions for the period following World War II. Yet, he stressed, international postwar peace and stability would depend on America's global leadership.

These moralistic pronouncements were meanwhile being matched by the zeal of American missionaries, especially in China. There the United States had promulgated an Open Door policy, designed to uphold China's sovereignty against the intrusions of European imperialists. But the missionaries were supposed to work from within to transform China into a Christian nation, thereby spurring the development of its democratic institutions and cementing its ties to America. Quaint though it may seem today, many prominent Americans hoped for a Christian China. Anson Burlingame, a U.S. diplomat and later adviser to the Manchu court, envisioned "the shining cross on every hill and in every valley" of China, and statesman William Jennings Bryan looked forward to a "new Chinese civilization . . . founded upon the Christian movement." Reveries of this kind heightened in the early 1930s, when Generalissimo Chiang Kai-shek, the Chinese Nationalist leader, converted to a Methodist sect—largely to improve his connections with the West. Many Americans soon saw China becoming a replica of the United States, a hope solemnly expressed by Senator Kenneth Wherry of Nebraska in 1940: "With God's help, we will lift Shanghai up and up, ever up, until it is just like Kansas City."

Exalting the same theme, Henry Luce, the influential proprietor of *Time* and *Life* magazines, unveiled a grand design for America's future on the eve of World War II. He was the son of missionaries and had been born in China. His essay in *Life*, "The American Century," struck a messianic tone: "We need most of all to seek and to bring forth a vision of America as a world power, which is authentically American. . . . America as the dynamic center of ever-widening spheres of enterprise, America as the training center of the skilled servants of mankind, America as the Good Samaritan, really believing again that it is more blessed to give than to receive, and America as the powerhouse of the ideals of Freedom and Justice—out of these elements surely can be fashioned a vision of the 20th century . . . the first great American Century."

Skepticism, even derision, greeted this oracular screed. Luce recanted—particularly in the face of a reply from the eminent theologian Reinhold Niebuhr, who warned against the "egoistic corruption" of nations propelled by such expectations. But the conviction voiced by Luce—the gospel of America's duty to preserve global order—persisted. It acquired fresh urgency after World War II, as the specter of monolithic communism haunted the United States. Over and over again, successive Presidents would explain their foreign policy in cosmic language. "The world today looks to us for leadership," said President Harry S Truman, and President Dwight D. Eisenhower spoke in similar terms. So did Kennedy, promising in his inaugural address that America would "pay any price, bear any burden, meet any hardship, support any friend, oppose any foe, to assure the survival and the success of liberty." Johnson's goal, as he described it, was to "bring peace and hope to all the peoples of the world," and President Richard M. Nixon portrayed himself as the architect of an international "structure of peace."

The United States thus proceeded on assumptions shared by the government and the public in an atmosphere of bipartisan consensus. The great strategic debates of the postwar period— such as "massive retaliation" versus "flexible response"—focused on means rather than aims. Accordingly, the American involvement in Vietnam was not a quagmire into which the United States stumbled blindly, even less the result of a conspiracy perpetrated by a cabal of warmongers in the White House, the Pentagon, or the State Department. Nor was the nation's slide into the Vietnam war predetermined by historical forces beyond the control of mortals. Legions of civilian and military bureaucrats, armed with tons of data, drafted and discussed plans and options which the President carefully weighed before making choices. The procedure was slow, meticulous, cumbersome, often agonizing.

Inexorably, the decisions reflected America's idea of its global role—a view that the United States could not recoil from world leadership. With the end of the war in Vietnam, however, that view dimmed. The "American Century," Daniel Bell has written, "foundered on the shoals of Vietnam." What remained, as seen in the electorate's support for President Ronald Reagan's vow to rebuild the nation's strength, was nostalgia.

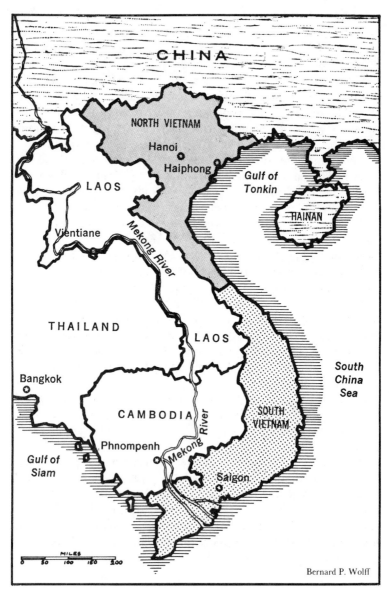

The 1954 Geneva agreements ended 60 years of French occupation and temporarily partitioned Vietnam at the 17th parallel.

2

Americans at War

Reappraisals of wars tend to be a litany of "what-might-have-beens" which profit from the acuity of hindsight, and the Vietnam experience is no exception. Most Americans canvassed in the spring of 1965, as Lyndon Johnson sent U.S. ground troops into battle for the first time, supported the commitment. After the war was over, however, Americans overwhelmingly repudiated the intervention as having been a blunder. But roughly the same proportion of the nation holds in retrospect that, once involved, the United States ought to have deployed all its power to succeed. Postwar opinion polls show that Americans blame their political leaders for denying victory to the U.S. forces in Vietnam by imposing restraints on their actions. A survey conducted in 1980 for the Veterans' Administration disclosed that 82 percent of former U.S. soldiers engaged in heavy combat there believe that the war was lost because they were not allowed to win—and, astonishingly, 66 percent indicated a willingness to fight again, presumably under fewer limitations. Looking back, too, many senior American officers who served in Vietnam predictably assert that defeat could have been averted had the war been waged more effectively.

In spring 1965 President Johnson sent the first U.S. ground forces into battle in South Vietnam. Above, U.S. marines splash ashore at Danang.

General William C. Westmoreland, who commanded the U.S. forces in Vietnam from 1965 to 1968, compiled a catalogue of grievances in his memoirs. He criticized President Johnson for intensifying the war effort too slowly, refusing to approve incursions against enemy sanctuaries in Laos and Cambodia, giving the South Vietnamese army inadequate equipment, and, among other things, succumbing to the vagaries of domestic opinion by "failing to level" with the American people. He also faulted President Nixon and his national security adviser, Henry Kissinger, for having "abandoned" the South Vietnamese regime by conceding to a cease-fire accord in January 1973 that permitted North Vietnamese troops to remain in the south. Above all, he denounced American television networks and newspapers for alleged distortions that supposedly turned the people against the war. "A lesson to be learned," he told me in retrospect, "is that young men should never be sent into battle unless the country is going to support them."

Other American military officers are equally troubled as they reassess the war. Like Westmoreland, they rail against the news media, contending that American reporters in Vietnam exaggerated setbacks and atrocities, and thus poisoned opinion at home. For many, though, the culprit was President Johnson, who deliberately declined to rally the U.S. public behind the war effort out of fear that mobilizing the country would doom his domestic economic and social programs. Therefore, they argue, the public's growing disaffection with the conflict eventually disillusioned the American forces in the field. General Fred Weyand, the last American commander in Vietnam, has said, "The American army is really a people's army in the sense that it belongs to the American people, who take a jealous and proprietary interest in its involvement. When the army is committed, the American people are committed; when the American people lose their commitment, it is futile to try to keep the army committed."

But the professionals also express resentment against their own superiors, and some even argue that the joint chiefs of staff should have resigned in protest against the strictures placed on their prosecution of the war. Air Force officers assert, for instance, that full-scale American bombing of North Vietnam from the start would have crushed the enemy. Infantry officers indict the rotation system, under which American troops spent only a year in Vietnam, hardly long enough to develop the *esprit de corps* that boosts morale and combat performance. To retired Brigadier General Robert Montague, who first went to Vietnam in the early 1960s, a crucial error was to have pitched conventional American units, trained to repel Russian aggression in Western Europe, into an unfamiliar terrain of jungles and rice fields, where Vietcong guerrillas could not be distinguished from Vietnamese peasants. Admiral Thomas H. Moorer, a former chairman of the joint chiefs of staff, insisted to me in his damn-the-torpedoes style that the war was waged in the wrong place: "We should have fought in the north, where everyone was the enemy, where you didn't have to worry whether or not you were shooting friendly civilians. In the south, we had to cope with women concealing grenades in their brassieres, or in their baby's diapers. I remember two of our marines being killed by a youngster whom they were teaching to play volleyball. But Lyndon Johnson didn't want to overthrow the North Vietnamese government. Well, the only reason to go to war is to overthrow a government you don't like."

Colonel Harry G. Summers Jr., an instructor at the Army War College, has concluded that the United States won a tactical victory but suffered a strategic failure in Vietnam. A veteran of two tours there, he is less critical of the politicians and the press than many of his fellow officers. He suggests that the basic mistake made by U.S. military planners was to have focused on chasing Vietcong guerrillas, who were deployed to grind down the American forces until big North Vietnamese units were ready to launch major operations. In other words, the Americans exhausted themselves in a costly, futile counterinsurgency effort—"like a bull charging the toreador's cape rather than the toreador." This was Westmoreland's "war of attrition," predicated on the theory that immensely superior U.S. firepower would ultimately wipe out the enemy. "You know," Summers told a North Vietnamese colonel after the war, "you never defeated us on the battlefield." To which his Communist counterpart replied, "That may be so, but it is also irrelevant."

Summers asserts that the Americans should have gone on the offensive late in 1965, after they spoiled a Communist attempt to cut across South Vietnam from the central highlands to the populated areas along the coast. He would have driven through the zone that separated North from South Vietnam, then pushed into neighboring Laos as far as the Thai border on the Mekong River in order to seal off the enemy infiltration routes running southward. That alternative, Summers believes, would have required fewer American troops than Westmoreland's grueling "search and destroy" missions, and reduced American losses. The task of fighting the Vietcong guerrillas, in his estimation, should have been relegated to the South Vietnamese army.

But such autopsies are academic exercises, like war games. The essential reality of the struggle was that the Communists, imbued with an almost fanatical sense of dedication to a reunified Vietnam under their control, saw the war against the United States and its South Vietnamese ally as the continuation of 2,000 years of resistance to Chinese and later French rule. They were prepared to accept limitless casualties to attain their sacred objective. Ho Chi Minh, their leader, had made that calculation plain to the French as they braced for war in the late 1940s. "You can kill ten of my men for every one I kill of yours," he warned them, "but even at those odds, you will lose and I will win." "Every minute, hundreds of thousands of people die on this earth," General Vo Nguyen Giap, the Communist commander, once said, and he discounted "the life or death of a hundred, a thousand, tens of thousands of human beings, even our compatriots." During the war against the Americans, he spoke of fighting 10, 15, 20, 50 years, regardless of cost, until "final victory."

American strategists misgauged the North Vietnamese and Vietcong by applying their own values to them. Westmoreland, for example, reckoned that he knew the threshold of their endurance: by "bleeding" them, he would awaken their leaders to the realization that they were draining their population "to the point of national disaster for generations," and thus compel them to sue for peace. Even after the war, he still seemed to have misunderstood the phenomenal discipline and determination of the North Vietnamese. "Any American commander who took the same vast losses as General Giap," he said, "would have been sacked overnight."

Many of the American civilians and soldiers who served in Vietnam were aware of the enemy's perseverance. Patrick J. McGarvey, a Central Intelligence Agency (CIA) analyst, noted in 1969 that no price was too high for Giap as long as he could ravage the American forces, since he measured the situation not by his casualties but by "the traffic in homebound American coffins." Konrad Kellen, a Rand Corporation expert, reached the same conclusion. "Short of being physically destroyed," he wrote of the Communists, "collapse, surrender, or disintegration was—to put it bizarrely—simply not within their capabilities." Lieutenant Colonel Stuart Herrington, a U.S. military adviser in Hau Nghia province in 1971 and 1972, recalled that he "couldn't help admiring the tenacity, aggressiveness, and bravery" of the North Vietnamese troops, who sincerely believed that they were "saving their southern brethren from the clutches of imperialism." An American general who prefers to remain anonymous called them "the best enemy we have faced in our history."

The enemy's intransigence was grotesquely apparent during the war in the spectacle of North Vietnamese and Vietcong corpses stacked up like cordwood following battles. In Vietnam after the war, I interviewed Communist veterans who had spent seven or eight or nine years fighting in the south, their jungle sanctuaries constantly pounded by U.S. bombs and artillery. When I asked them to describe their motives, all replied almost by rote that it had been their duty to "liberate the fatherland." The slogan sounded contrived to my skeptical ears. Yet, as I listened to them, I thought of the old Mathew Brady photographs of Union and Confederate bodies at Antietam and Manassas and Gettysburg, where thousands of young men had also sacrificed themselves. Theirs had been a cause Americans could comprehend.

Only much later did American officials begin to recognize that the United States had faced a formidable foe. Dean Rusk, secretary of state under Kennedy and Johnson, whose devotion to the anti-Communist crusade in Southeast Asia dated back to the years of the Truman Administration, finally admitted in 1971 that he had "personally underestimated" the ability of the North Vietnamese to resist. "They've taken over 700,000 killed, which in relation to population is almost the equivalent of—what? Ten million Americans?" General Maxwell D. Taylor, who had contributed to Kennedy's decisions on Vietnam and afterward served as Johnson's ambassador in Saigon, had a similar confession to make after the war: "First, we didn't know ourselves. We thought we were going into another Korean war, but this was a different country. Secondly, we didn't know our South Vietnamese allies. We never understood them, and that was another surprise. And we knew even less about North Vietnam. Who was Ho Chi Minh? Nobody really knew. So, until we know the enemy and know our allies and know ourselves, we'd better keep out of this dirty kind of business. It's very dangerous."

President Nixon's chief foreign policy aide, Henry Kissinger, was also baffled and frustrated by the Communists during his secret negotiations with them. Kissinger had tried above all to avoid a repetition of the inconclusive Korean war armistice talks, which had dragged on for two years because, he believed, America had not stiffened its diplomacy with the threat of force. He calculated that the North Vietnamese would compromise only if menaced with total annihilation—an approach that Nixon privately dubbed his "madman theory." But, like his predecessors, Kissinger never found their breaking point. His later claims to the contrary, the Communists agreed to a cease-fire in October 1972 only after he had handed them major concessions that were to jeopardize the future of the South Vietnamese government.

The real pressure on the Nixon Administration to reach a settlement in Vietnam came from the American public, which by that time wanted peace at almost any price—for reasons that Kissinger himself had perceived four years before. Early in 1968, on the eve of Tet, the Asian lunar New Year, the Communists had launched a dramatic offensive against towns and cities throughout South Vietnam, which Kissinger saw as the "watershed" of the American effort in Vietnam: "Henceforth, no matter how effective our actions, the prevalent strategy could no longer achieve its objectives within a period or with force levels politically acceptable to the American people."

Americans had been prepared to make sacrifices in blood and treasure, as they had in other wars. But they had to be shown progress, told when the war would end. In World War II, they could trace the advance of their army across Europe; in Vietnam, where there were no fronts, they were only given meaningless enemy "body counts"—and promises. So the United States, which had brought to bear stupendous military power to crack Communist morale, itself shattered under the strain of a struggle

Antiwar protesters in New York City's financial district, summer 1969

that seemed to be interminable. An original aim of the intervention, first enunciated by President Eisenhower, had been to protect all of Southeast Asia, whose countries would presumably "topple like a row of dominoes" were the Communists to take over Vietnam. Ironically, as Leslie Gelb of *The New York Times* observed, the real domino to fall was American public opinion.

The public, distressed by mounting casualties, rising taxes, and no prospect of a solution in sight, turned against the war long before America's political leaders did. Doubts had crept over many members of Congress. Yet except for a handful of senators, among them William Fulbright, Wayne Morse, Ernest Gruening, Gaylord Nelson, and Eugene McCarthy, few translated their private misgivings into open dissent. Not until March 1968, when he decided to run for the presidency, did John F. Kennedy's brother Robert, the senator from New York, denounce the American commitment to South Vietnam—having initially been one of its vocal advocates. Nor was there much dissidence at the upper echelons of the Executive branch, apart from George Ball, a senior State Department figure during the Kennedy and Johnson Administrations. Ball later looked back on the war as "probably the greatest single error made by America in its history." Robert S. McNamara, who served both Kennedy and Johnson as defense secretary, may have done more than any other individual to mold U.S. policy in Vietnam, but he lost confidence by late 1967 and came close to an emotional breakdown. He has remained silent on the subject since then.

McNamara's successor, Clark M. Clifford, had been a strong proponent of a vigorous military approach to Vietnam before taking charge of the Defense Department. A sensitive political animal, his antennae sharply attuned to the national mood, he changed overnight, and played the decisive part in persuading President Johnson to alter his course. In 1981, as I interviewed him in his luxurious Washington law office, he tried to put the Vietnam experience in perspective: "Countries, like human beings, make mistakes. We made an honest mistake. I feel no sense of shame. Nor should the country feel any sense of shame. We felt that we were doing what was necessary. It proved to be unsound."

Such admissions scarcely console the South Vietnamese, who by 1973 had discovered to their dismay that America, after 20 years, would not wage the war indefinitely. Bui Diem, who served as South Vietnam's ambassador to the United States and remained in America, draws a broader lesson from the phenomenon: "Small nations must be wary of the Americans, since U.S. policies shift quickly as domestic politics and public opinion change. The struggle for us was a matter of life or death. But, for the Americans, it was merely an unhappy chapter in their history, and they could turn the page. We were allied, yet we had different interests."

Fortunately, the Vietnam failure has not gripped the United States in a torment of recrimination of the kind that followed China's fall to communism. No congressional committees have staged inquisitions of allegedly "un-American" citizens. Nor has a demagogue emerged to match Senator Joseph R. McCarthy, whose cynical witch-hunts in the 1950s put a generation on trial. Despite his portrayal of the struggle as a "noble cause" betrayed by politicians, President Reagan refrained from making it an issue. Perhaps the turmoil that convulsed the nation during the war left Americans too exhausted to embark on a quest for blame. Or perhaps the trauma was so profound that they prefer to forget. Yet, as Kissinger says, "Vietnam is still with us. It has created doubts about American judgment, about American credibility, about American power—not only at home, but throughout the world. It has poisoned our domestic debate. So we paid an exorbitant price for the decisions that were made in good faith and for good purpose."

Few places in America paid as high a price as did Bardstown, a Kentucky community of 7,000, 16 of whose boys died in the war. Early in 1983, a decade after the last American troops left Vietnam, a CBS television team visited Bardstown to capture its postwar mood. "I personally can't see that we accomplished anything," said one veteran, and another added: "A lot of people want to make sure that we don't engage in that type of situation again." Gus Wilson, mayor when the young men departed with their national guard unit in 1968, was still mayor: "We believed that the first thing that you did for your country was to defend it. You didn't question that. But I think we realized as we went along—maybe later than we should have—that the government was pulling a bit of a flimflam. We weren't getting the truth. The Vietnam war was being misrepresented to the people—the way it was conducted, its ultimate purpose. Though I'm still a patriot, I ended up very disillusioned."

Millions of Americans share Gus Wilson's sentiment. And their collective disenchantment, known as the Vietnam syndrome, has restrained U.S. leaders from undertaking hazardous ventures since the war ended. Had it not been for Vietnam, the Carter Administration might have maneuvered either openly or covertly to thwart the advance of leftist movements in Ethiopia and Angola, or to save the shah of Iran from collapse. Both President

Reagan and the Congress went through a tortured debate before committing U.S. marines to a multinational peacekeeping force in Lebanon. The fear of entanglement in another jungle conflict has also ranged the American people squarely against involvement in the crises testing Central America. Indeed, the divergent attitudes of Americans toward the rebellion in El Salvador today and the growing insurgency in South Vietnam two decades ago exemplify the dramatic difference.

By the end of 1963, American assistance to South Vietnam was costing $400 million annually. Some 12,000 military advisers were serving there, and 50 of them had been killed during the four previous years—even though their assignment theoretically prohibited their engagement in battle. Yet a poll published at the time disclosed that 63 percent of Americans were paying "little or no attention" to the situation. Nor did Vietnam cause much worry on Capitol Hill. In August 1964, the Congress passed the Tonkin Gulf resolution with barely a murmur of dissent, thereby giving President Johnson what one of his aides was to call "the functional equivalent of a declaration of war." The nation's lack of interest in Vietnam then was equally apparent in the fact that, until the U.S. marines splashed ashore in the spring of 1965, only five American news organizations maintained staff correspondents in Saigon.

Contrast the disregard for Vietnam then with America's jittery focus on El Salvador later. Though only 55 U.S. military advisers were serving there in early 1983, American regulations tightly circumscribed their activities in order to avoid incidents that might exacerbate apprehensions at home. The rules barred them from participating in Salvadoran army operations or even from carrying weapons larger than a revolver—and, in February 1983, three American officers discovered on a combat mission were unceremoniously relieved of their duties. Congress bluntly rebuffed President Reagan's first secretary of state, General Alexander M. Haig Jr., when he attempted to step up the U.S. involvement in Central America in 1981. Opinion surveys two years later divulged that 59 percent of Americans opposed the presence of military advisers in El Salvador, and 72 percent disapproved of an increase in U.S. military aid to the Salvadoran government. Paradoxically, a majority of Americans agreed that a Communist takeover of El Salvador would jeopardize the security of the United States, but that risk seemed to be preferable to American intervention. David Reichhart, a Michigan schoolteacher, told a *New York Times* interviewer: "I don't want communism to come into this hemisphere, but I don't think the people of this country should be responsible for having to go in and fight."

The echo of Vietnam resonates through these recent surveys. By a margin of two to one, respondents to a *Washington Post* study replied in 1982 that they foresaw El Salvador becoming another Vietnam, and the analogy pervaded a *New York Times* poll. "Vietnam went on year after year," said Carl W. Koch Jr., of Collingswood, New Jersey, "and I'm afraid that we'll get into El Salvador in the same way." Dennis F. Leary, a Massachusetts air-conditioner repairman, expressed the fear that "maybe we'll take it too lightly, like we did in Vietnam"; "we shouldn't put troops on the line if we're not ready to back them one hundred percent." Mingled in this nervousness, too, was a hint of the isolationism that had permeated America before World War II propelled the nation into assuming global obligations. "It seems like we're always getting pulled in by other people's problems," remarked Cynthia Crone of Payne, Ohio. "We've got enough problems of our own to deal with."

Even if Vietnam had not shaken public confidence in America's role in world affairs, the United States was in no condition following the war to play international gendarme. For the struggle had, along with its other casualties, ruined the nation's military establishment. As late as 1980, Army Chief of Staff General Edward C. Meyer warned Congress that he was presiding over a "hollow" force—short of personnel, experience, and equipment.

The U.S. Army in Vietnam was a shambles as the war drew to a close in the early 1970s. With President Nixon then repatriating the Americans, nobody wanted to be the last to perish for a

Masked demonstrators parade along Central Park in New York City.

cause that had clearly lost its meaning, and the name of the game for those awaiting withdrawal was survival. Antiwar protests at home had by now spread to the men in the field, many of whom wore peace symbols and refused to go into combat. Race relations, which were good when blacks and whites had earlier shared a sense of purpose, became increasingly brittle. The use of drugs was so widespread that, according to an official estimate made in 1971, nearly one third of the troops were addicted to opium or heroin, and marijuana smoking had become routine. Soldiers not only disobeyed their superiors but, in an alarming number of incidents, actually murdered them with fragmentation grenades—a practice dubbed "fragging." An ugly scandal surfaced after officers and noncoms were arraigned for reaping personal profits from service clubs and post exchanges. Morale also deteriorated following revelations of a massacre in which a U.S. infantry company slaughtered more than 300 Vietnamese inhabitants of Mylai village in cold blood—an episode that prompted GIs to assume that their commanders were covering up other atrocities.

American strategists were appalled by the broader impact of the struggle on the U.S. Armed Forces. Between 1965 and the departure of the last American combat soldier in early 1973, the bill for Vietnam had totaled more than $120 billion—much of which would have normally been invested in the modernization of the nation's defenses. As a result, America's security structure had in several respects become an anachronism, its divisions in Western Europe no match for their Warsaw Pact adversaries, in either skill or weapons. Moreover, Johnson's reluctance to increase taxes or to impose economic controls to pay for the Vietnam war had caused inflation that the Arab oil embargo of 1973 compounded; the costs of rebuilding the American military establishment soared. By 1975, U.S. defense spending in real terms was roughly $4 billion per year lower than it had been a decade earlier. But inflation was not the only factor.

Nixon ended an inequitable and unpopular draft in order to curry favor with voters. He regretted the move later—as would military professionals and many political figures, both conservative and liberal. For one thing, GI salaries had to be raised to competitive civilian levels to encourage enlistments, and soon the defense budget was consumed by wages. Volunteers were also attracted from among the underprivileged and undereducated—young men often least qualified to handle a modern army's sophisticated technology. Hostility to the war had damaged university and college reserve officer training programs, whose enrollments dropped precipitously from more than 200,000 in 1968 to some 75,000 by 1973. An important source of bright, innovative, open-minded leadership narrowed, leaving much of the army's management to superannuated bureaucrats.

American military planners were also influenced by their observations of the Yom Kippur war fought in the Sinai desert between Israel and Egypt at the end of 1973. That collision portended the kind of conflict that the United States might face in Europe—a confrontation waged in open terrain by large infantry units dependent on tanks, tactical missiles, and transport helicopters. As a consequence, they downgraded the counterinsurgency doctrines that had been designed to check guerrillas in the jungles of Asia, Africa, and Latin America and returned to conventional concepts. In the decade since, the American army has regained much of its former strength—though, as General Meyer points out, it is still a force "in transition."

Its social profile has changed. More than 85 percent of army volunteers in 1982 were high school graduates, compared to 67 percent two years before. The economic slump stimulated enlistments among the jobless, who preferred a relatively well-paid stint in uniform to unemployment, and recruiters shifted their drives away from black ghettos to the white suburbs, where they had surprising success in signing up middle-class youths. And, while the memory of Vietnam is still fresh, military service has again acquired a measure of respectability in American eyes. But the army trailed the Reagan Administration's list of defense priorities, far behind the development of a strategic nuclear arsenal.

The image of the Vietnam veteran may have benefited from the gradual renewal in public esteem for the armed forces, and it clearly did from the monument in Washington. Yet many veterans feel themselves to be members of a dislocated generation, their place in the society uncomfortable, undefined, almost embarrassing—as if the nation has projected onto them its own sense of guilt or shame or humiliation for the war. Portrayals of the Vietnam veteran in the news media are frequently two-dimensional distortions. He is neither the junkie strumming a guitar in a California commune nor the bustling huckster making millions in Houston real estate. Most GIs returned from Vietnam quietly and unobtrusively, blending back into the population. But the war crippled an unusually high proportion of them, physically and mentally, in ways that are not quickly visible.

Thousands of soldiers in Vietnam were exposed to Agent Orange, a chemical herbicide, which may have afflicted them with cancer, skin disease, and other disorders. A Veterans' Administration psychiatrist, Dr. Jack Ewalt, estimates that some 700,000 vets suffer from various forms of "posttraumatic stress disorder," the modern term for "shell shock" in World War I and "battle fatigue" in World War II. Vietnam caused many more cases than those conflicts, however. Its symptoms, which can occur 10 or even 15 years later, range from panic and rage to anxiety, depression, and emotional paralysis. Crime, suicide, alcoholism, narcotics addiction, divorce, and unemployment among Vietnam veterans far outstrip the norm. A massive study published in 1981 by the Center for Policy Research and the City University of New York concluded that those who served in Vietnam "are plagued by significantly more problems than their peers."

War is war. Why was Vietnam distinctive?

The danger was pervasive and chronic. I spent three years in the army during World War II, much of the time at airfields and supply depots in northeastern India, without ever hearing a shot. But there were no secure areas in Vietnam. A GI assigned to an office in Saigon or a warehouse in Danang could be killed or injured at any moment of the day or night by Communist mortars or rockets. And during his one-year tour an infantryman humping the bush was in combat almost continually—harassed by enemy mines, booby traps, and snipers if not engaged in direct clashes. Philip Caputo, one of the more eloquent chroniclers of the Vietnam war, has noted by comparison that U.S. marine units, celebrated for their exploits against the Japanese in the Pacific campaign, fought for no longer than six or eight weeks during all of World War II.

The average age of the American soldier in Vietnam was 19, 7 years younger than his father had been in World War II, which made him more vulnerable to the psychological strains of the struggle—strains that were aggravated by the special tension of Vietnam, where every peasant might be a Vietcong terrorist. William Ehrhart, a former marine, recalled a flash of the past that, years after the war, still haunts his dreams: "Whenever you turned around, you'd be taking it in the solar plexus. Then the enemy would disappear, and you'd end up taking out your frustrations on the civilians. The way we operated, any Vietnam-

February 1965: Captured insurgents are evacuated from a rice field and loaded into a U.S. Army helicopter by South Vietnamese troops.

ese seen running away from Americans was a Vietcong suspect, and we could shoot. It was standard operating procedure. One day I shot a woman in a rice field because she was running—just running away from the Americans. And I killed her. Fifty-five or sixty years old, unarmed, and at the time I didn't even think twice about it."

Paradoxically, the wonders of modern science contributed to the plight of Vietnam veterans. Medical helicopters were so fast and efficient that a GI wounded in action could be on an operating table within 15 minutes. Statistics tell the story. During World War II, roughly one out of every four U.S. marine casualties died. But survivors in Vietnam outnumbered the dead by a ratio of seven to one, and men who might have perished on the battlefield are now alive—often invalids in need of constant care.

American soldiers in other wars gauged progress by conquering territory; seizing the next town on the route to victory sustained their morale. In Vietnam, by contrast, GIs captured and recaptured the same ground, and not even the generals could explain the aim of the fighting. The only measure of success was the "body count," the pile of enemy slaughtered—a futile standard that made the war as glorious as an abattoir. So homecoming troops were often denounced for bestiality or berated for the defeat—or simply shunned. John Kerry, later elected lieutenant-governor of Massachusetts, recalled his return: "There I was, a week out of the jungle, flying from San Francisco to New York. I fell asleep and woke up yelling, probably a nightmare. The other passengers moved away from me—a reaction I noticed more and more in the months ahead. The country didn't give a shit about the guys coming back, or what they'd gone through. The feeling toward them was, 'Stay away—don't contaminate us with whatever you've brought back from Vietnam.' "

Different veterans bear different grievances. Some want more assistance, improved counseling, better jobs. Others continue to wage the war or protest against it; many are still striving to understand what happened. Above all, they seem to be seeking respect and justice—the debt that nations owe their warriors. Monuments and parades and requiems may not be enough.

3

Postwar Vietnam

A merica's postwar troubles pale in comparison to conditions in Vietnam, which I revisited for seven weeks in early 1981—the longest stay authorized by the Communist government to any U.S. journalist since the shooting stopped six years before. I rediscovered a land not only ravaged by a generation of almost uninterrupted conflict, but governed by an inept and repressive regime incompetent to cope with the challenge of recovery.

Rebuilding Vietnam would have been a stupendous task under the best of circumstances. The war shattered its economy, disrupted its social texture, and exhausted its population in both the north and the south. But the Communists, showing the same intransigence that inspired them to resist the tremendous U.S. military machine, committed blunders that ruined their chances of winning the peace. Today one of the most impoverished places on earth, Vietnam faces bleak prospects. Prime Minister Pham Van Dong admitted as much as we chatted in French in an ornate salon of a Hanoi mansion that had once housed France's colonial governor. An energetic septuagenarian whose entire life has been devoted to struggle, he appeared to be overwhelmed by Vietnam's present circumstances: "Yes, we defeated the United States. But now we are plagued by problems. We do not have enough to eat. We are a poor, underdeveloped nation. *Vous savez,* waging a war is simple, but running a country is very difficult."

In 1977, Pham Van Dong and his comrades squandered an opportunity to establish diplomatic ties with the United States. Secretary of State Cyrus R. Vance and one of his chief aides, Richard C. Holbrooke, were keen to grant American recognition to Vietnam as a step toward a reconciliation, and President Jimmy Carter favored the move. But Holbrooke promptly ran into a stone wall when the negotiations started in Paris. The Vietnamese insisted, as a precondition, on some $3 billion in "war reparations"—and cited a secret pledge of this aid to them by President Nixon in early 1973 as an incentive to sign the cease-fire agreement. Nixon's promise, which lacked the approval of Congress, was probably illegal, but the Vietnamese stubbornly clung to their demand, having absurdly factored the potential sum into their economic plans. Late in 1978, realizing their miscalculation, they reversed themselves. By then, however, the propitious moment had passed.

At that stage, President Carter's national security adviser, Zbigniew Brzezinski, was eager to taunt the Soviet Union by elevating America's quasi-official relationship with China to a formal level of diplomatic recognition. He argued that a rapprochement with Vietnam would damage the more important Sino-American connection, since the Vietnamese were then antagonizing the Chinese by edging closer to the Soviet Union. Carter's domestic political advisers backed Brzezinski, contending that U.S. public opinion was still hostile to Vietnam—partly because its government had been uncooperative in delivering the remains of more than 2,000 Americans missing in action during the war. Meanwhile, thousands of refugees were beginning to flee Vietnam by sea, and the agony of the "boat people" attracted worldwide attention. And U.S. intelligence devices detected reliable signs of an impending Vietnamese invasion of Cambodia. Plans for the American recognition of Vietnam were shelved, and they are still gathering dust.

36,000 "boat people" from Vietnam were given temporary shelter in the Pilau Bidong refugee camp in Malaysia in 1979.

United Nations/Photo by J.K. Isaac

Because of their mistake, the Vietnamese forfeited American aid, which almost surely would have been forthcoming in one form or another had they established relations with the United States. American loans and investment, bolstered by trade with the United States, would have helped to stimulate the Vietnamese economy—and make it less dependent on the Soviet Union, whose assistance program of about a billion dollars a year is tightly controlled. But the Vietnamese have not given up hope. On more than one occasion during my weeks in Hanoi, my guide pointed to a large gray villa on Hai Ba Trung Street, a busy downtown thoroughfare, reminding me somewhat sorrowfully that it had been cleaned and renovated and its rats exterminated, awaiting the U.S. diplomatic mission that may never arrive.

When the Communists finally conquered Saigon on April 30, 1975, the North Vietnamese officer who took the government's surrender, Colonel Bui Tin, reassured South Vietnamese officials that they had nothing to fear. "All Vietnamese are the victors and only the American imperialists have been vanquished," he told them. "If you love the nation and the people, consider today a happy day." But soon afterward, the Communists proceeded to shunt 400,000 South Vietnamese civil servants and army officers as well as doctors, lawyers, teachers, journalists, and other intellectuals into "re-education" centers—and the concentration camps still hold between 50,000 and a 100,000 people.

There are about 40 of these camps in the south, several of them jails once used by the Saigon regime to detain its critics. The inmates are reported to suffer from malnutrition, malaria, dysentery, and other diseases as a result of inadequate food and medical care, and accounts of torture and summary executions abound. At one large center, located near the town of Tan Hiep, south of Saigon, those charged with infractions of the rules are beaten and shackled in the sun without water. Elsewhere, they are locked in the same "tiger cages" that the South Vietnamese government employed to incarcerate its dissidents—and which aroused protests in America during the war. Ironically, many of the present prisoners, opponents of the Saigon authorities, initially welcomed and later annoyed the Communists, and they include Vietcong veterans. The system may be less savage than the methods of Stalin and Mao Zedong, who slaughtered millions of their adversaries. But it has been denounced by Amnesty International, an organization that monitors human rights violations.

Apart from its inhumanity, Vietnamese repression betrays Vietnam's own interests by discarding the skilled people needed for national recovery. During my visit to Ho Chi Minh City, as Saigon was renamed after the war, I encountered a former professor of medicine recently released from a camp. He and his wife, a lawyer, both intense nationalists, had deliberately remained in Vietnam after the Communist takeover in hopes of contributing to their country's reconstruction. Now, their spirit broken, they dream of escape. Many young engineers, accountants, economists, and other technicians have disappeared into "re-education" centers simply because they were educated in America or had held jobs in the discredited South Vietnamese government. A northern Communist official stationed in the south defended the purge, asserting to me that "we must get rid of the bourgeois rubbish." But Dr. Duong Quynh Hoa, a pediatrician who had played a prominent role in the Vietcong, took a different view. "The ideologues are in command," she told me. "We are wasting our best talent."

Antiquated Marxist ideology also prompted the Vietnamese leaders to commit an egregious error immediately after the war, when they launched a five-year plan that concentrated on developing such heavy industries as steel, chemicals, and cement at the expense of agriculture. Under the plan, ample supplies of food would flow from collective farms as peasants dedicated themselves to producing for the state. But the Communist regime could not generate investment capital for industrial development—partly because of its inability to export and also because Nixon's promised "war reparations" never materialized. Its expectation of fat revenues from offshore petroleum also fizzled, when West German, Italian, Canadian, and French oil companies, hamstrung by bureaucratic red tape, dropped their exploration projects. At the same time, farm output faltered, particularly in the fertile Mekong delta, where peasants accustomed to tilling their own soil resisted collectivization. Villagers in many places killed their water buffalo and oxen rather than have them confiscated, and they left large tracts fallow rather than cultivate rice for the government. The five-year plan proved to be disastrous, and the economy has barely improved since.

The rice harvest, scheduled to reach 21 million tons annually in 1980, was still 5 million tons below that target three years later. The official cereal ration during my stay in Vietnam was about 30 pounds per month—and it consisted mostly of wheat, tapioca, and other starches which the Vietnamese detest. Even so, it was five pounds less than the minimum recommended by the World

Health Organization, and this was virtually the only item in the Vietnamese diet. Fish, the main protein, has been scarce because fishermen lack fuel and nets—and because thousands of refugees have fled aboard fishing boats—and meat is a rarity. "A whole generation will bear the stigmata of this famine all their lives," observed the late Dr. Ton That Tung in 1981, formerly Ho Chi Minh's personal physician. And Dr. Duong Quynh Hoa illustrated the crisis vividly to me at her hospital in Ho Chi Minh City. Its wards were packed with children on the brink of starvation, some lying two or three to a cot, others sleeping on the floor, their frail bodies bloated and stunted by hunger—a situation she described in French as *"invivable"*—almost the equivalent of hopeless—adding with a gesture of futility, "Where do we go from here?"

Vietnam's few industries operate in slow motion or not at all. The production of coal, once a major export, has sunk drastically because of a shortage of trucks, conveyers, and other machinery. Plastics factories have been shut down because there is no hard currency to import polyethylene, and other enterprises are paralyzed for lack of raw materials. The most ordinary goods, like soap or needles or envelopes, cannot be found in Hanoi, where the only department store is virtually empty. Inefficiency, confusion, pilferage, and venality are meanwhile endemic—at a heavy cost to the marginal economy.

About 30,000 tons of freight are landed daily at Haiphong, the nation's principal northern port, most of it aid from the Soviet Union and other Communist nations. But roughly half of it is stolen or left to rot on the wharves. During my visit there, I saw crates that had been unloaded upside down or broken, and equipment rusting from neglect. The components of a complete French cement plant, still in their containers, had been languishing on a dock for two years. The congestion is ghastly—and deliberate. Customs and harbor officials require bribes. Ships must also bribe the authorities to discharge their cargoes, and the illicit tariff is fixed. Japanese vessels, which can afford the top fee of $5,000, usually turn around in three or four days. The less affluent linger for a month, sometimes six months. International proletarian solidarity notwithstanding, Soviet and East European captains are hit for payoffs.

Overall, instead of expanding at a rate of 14 percent a year as envisioned under the ambitious five-year plan, the Vietnamese economy grew by only 2 percent annually—lagging behind a birthrate of 3 percent (one of the highest in the world) and prolonging a trend that has been going on for more than a half century. Despite wars, Vietnam's population has tripled since 1930, while its rice production has barely doubled in that time. The country's average income today is well under $200 a year, making it one of the poorest on earth. The rest of Asia is booming, but Vietnam remains an island of poverty—a tragedy given the ingenuity and industriousness of its people, who, spurred by incentives, might well match the dynamism of the South Koreans or the Taiwanese.

"It has always been a disaster for Vietnam to rely on one large friend," Pham Van Dong said a few years ago, referring to China, but the comment could also be applied to the Soviet Union. Vietnamese economic setbacks, together with antagonism to China and tensions with the United States, have propelled the Vietnamese squarely into the Soviet orbit.

The Soviets deliver Vietnam two essentials, oil and grain. They have assigned some 4,000 advisers to such projects as improving Vietnam's primitive railways and building electric power plants, and they underwrite the Vietnamese army of occupation in Cambodia. But they drive a hard bargain: they compel the Vietnamese to pay for the aid with handicrafts, raw materials, and other commodities, an arrangement that deprives Vietnam of items that might earn it hard currency in the West to buy the technology the Soviets cannot provide. The Soviets have also been known to resell the products on Western markets at lower prices than the Vietnamese quote, thereby undercutting their own dependents. Worse yet, the Vietnamese lack the goods to repay or even service the loans on schedule, and they are digging themselves deeper and deeper into debt to the Soviets, who refuse to sink more money into Vietnam.

Late in 1982, when a high-ranking Vietnamese delegation

went to Moscow to appeal for additional help, Leonid I. Brezhnev, the ailing Soviet president, spurned the plea on the grounds that he had "considerable programs" of his own to fund. Vietnam's No. 2 leader, Truong Chinh, who headed the group, emphasized that the Soviet Union had always fulfilled its "international obligations." But the Vietnamese went home without an extra ruble.

The Soviet Union has also taken advantage of its assistance to Vietnam to improve its strategic position in Asia. Its aircraft and warships now use the huge complex erected by the United States at Camranh Bay, but the Vietnamese have consistently rebuffed Soviet requests for permanent rights to the base. They recollect numerous instances in the past of Soviet disregard for their interests—such as the occasion in spring of 1972 when Brezhnev entertained Nixon handsomely in Moscow just as the United States was bombing Hanoi and mining Haiphong harbor for the first time. They were jittery in early 1983 as Brezhnev's successor, Yuri V. Andropov, resumed negotiations designed to reach a rapprochement with China, their prime enemy. Andropov manifested his priorities bluntly at Brezhnev's funeral—embracing the Chinese foreign minister and brushing off the official Vietnamese representatives.

Though far less obtrusive than Americans were during the war, the Soviet advisers currently in Vietnam are scarcely objects of admiration. The trim, delicate, supple Vietnamese seem to be almost physically repelled by their presence. The Russians resemble caricatures—big, beefy, sweaty men dressed in dowdy clothes unsuited to the tropical climate. I was reminded, as they wandered forlornly around Hanoi or Ho Chi Minh City, of the big, beefy, sweaty American hard-hats who used to work for American construction firms in Southeast Asia—but with a couple of differences. Tiny, tarty Vietnamese girls invariably flanked the Americans, while the Russians are usually accompanied by wives as hefty as themselves. The Americans exuded wealth, while the Russians look like muzhiks without two kopecks to rub together—much less spend lavishly in Vietnam.

Keenly aware of the distinction, the Vietnamese deride the Russians as "Americans without dollars." When I was in Hanoi, the Vietnamese were also retailing a joke that reflected both their disappointment with Soviet stinginess and their own destitution. Moscow, rejecting a desperate cry for help, cables Vietnam: "Tighten your belts." To which Vietnam replies: "Send belts."

The Vietnamese Communists blame America for their problems, contending that the United States has urged its allies to withhold assistance from Vietnam because of its invasion of Cambodia. And it is true that the Reagan Administration has been pressing various United Nations agencies to be stringent with Vietnam, a tactic that has succeeded. But, publicly and privately, Communist officials concede that they themselves are far more to blame for having failed to provide their people with the incentives to boost trade and production. Hoang Tung, the party propaganda boss, rambling on in impeccable French during a chat in his stuffy Hanoi office, acknowledged: "We made mistakes, and we've learned our lesson. We have not used economic levers. Our egalitarianism has sapped the enthusiasm of the workers."

Following a pivotal meeting in 1979, the Vietnamese Communists gingerly introduced flexible economic policies that made the term "profit motive" fashionable, even to their sectarian extremists. Peasants were allowed to cultivate their own crops and raise livestock for sale in free markets, as long as they fulfilled quotas that their collectives could negotiate with the government. Small merchants and artisans were permitted to function as private entrepreneurs, and state factories switched to paying their employees on a piecework basis—a practice once denounced by Marxists as a heinous capitalist evil. Vietnam's economic structure was decentralized in an effort to "widen the power and the responsibility of localities," as Le Duan, the Communist party chief, explained. The new system went into motion gradually, and it caused as many headaches as it was supposed to cure.

Their failures gave the Vietnamese leaders no plausible alternative to offering the material rewards that stimulate trade and production. A dilemma for a Communist regime, however, is to assure that the reforms that encourage workers, peasants, and merchants do not efface its authority. But by 1981, free-market forces were swiftly gathering momentum and eroding the Communist party's controls, and they have been unraveling at a rapid pace since then. A liberal economy requires abundance. With scarcities still severe, the reforms have led to spiraling inflation, mounting inequities, growing cynicism, widespread corruption, and a breakdown of the social, cultural, and political values that the Communists are determined to preserve. One Vietnamese official in Hanoi seemed to be almost nostalgic for the war as he recalled the days when the American bombing stiffened the resolve of the northern population. In Ho Chi Minh City, a Communist cadre said, "For most people, the only ideology that counts is a full stomach."

Nothing has dramatized the revulsion against poverty and repression more vividly than the massive exodus from Vietnam— one of the largest migrations of modern times. Nearly a million people have risked their lives to escape from the country, most by sea. Some 50,000 of them have died from exposure or drowning, or from attacks by pirates who traditionally maraud the waters off Southeast Asia. At least a half million men, women, and children have also fled from Cambodia and Laos, and all except 100,000 still languish in squalid camps along the borders of Thailand. Among the first to leave Vietnam were ethnic Chinese. Many of them, expelled when Vietnam and China clashed in early 1979, were fleeced by Vietnamese Communist officials as they departed. I interviewed several of these refugees as their weathered vessel landed at a Hong Kong wharf.

One, a carpenter, revealed that he and some friends had pooled their hoard of gold to make the voyage from the southern port of Danang for themselves and their families, about 60 people in all. They started by paying local Communist officials bribes amounting to some $2,000 to look the other way as they prepared for their trip. Then they bought a fishing boat and equipped it with an auxiliary engine and diesel fuel, an expenditure of $5,000

Vietnamese refugees, newly arrived in Kowloon, Hong Kong, await transfer to temporary camps.

United Nations/Photo by J.K. Isaac

more, and finally began the journey that was to take five weeks. The officials confiscated most of their belongings before they embarked, but they were lucky. Many boats crammed with refugees were intercepted by Vietnamese naval ships, whose officers snatched anything they could grab, including wedding rings. In some instances, the Communist authorities connived with Chinese racketeers to bilk the refugees.

4

Saigon Revisited

Saigon at the height of the war had stunk of decay. Its bars were drug centers, its hotels brothels, its boulevards and squares a sprawling black market hawking everything from sanitary napkins to rifles—all of it purloined from American warehouses. Soldiers from Ohio and Georgia and Oregon, black and white, their pockets filled with cash, strolled streets crowded with whores and pimps, beggars, orphans, cripples, and other victims of devastation. South Vietnamese army generals, enriched by silent Chinese partners, possessed gaudy villas not far from putrid slums packed with refugees, and government officials and businessmen connived constantly, shuffling and reshuffling the seemingly limitless flow of dollars. It was a city for sale—obsessed by greed, oblivious to its impending doom. Returning six years after the end of the war, I found it strangely the same, despite profound changes.

Some changes were cosmetic. The bars and brothels had been closed. The traffic clog of trucks and taxis and motor scooters was gone, and with it the choking gasoline fumes that had once pervaded the town. Like the city itself, streets and buildings had been renamed to herald the revolution. The Hôtel Caravelle, where foreign correspondents huddled during the war, had become the Doc Lap, or Independence, reserved for senior Communist functionaries. The main thoroughfare, Rue Catinat when I first arrived in Saigon in the 1950s, had been altered in the early 1960s to Tu Do, or Freedom. Now it was Dong Khoi, or Uprising, but everyone still called it Catinat. The U.S. embassy had been taken over by the Vietnamese government oil corporation, and the Communist army had seized the American military headquarters with much of its equipment intact. The airport, formerly as busy as Chicago's O'Hare, was asleep.

Within a day or so, though, I began to sniff deeper changes. When the Communists drove into Saigon in 1975, they were prudently greeted by a dazed population yearning for peace and prepared to cooperate. But instead of proceeding gently, they embarked on a program of wholesale repression, creating neighborhood committees of agents and informers to report on citizens, and arresting anyone even remotely affiliated with the *ancien régime*. Thus I sensed a city stifled by fear and cloaked in an eerie mood of melancholy—a ghostly place. And there were the ghosts of the people I had known before.

The bartender at the Hôtel Caravelle is a familiar face. "*C'est bien de vous revoir, monsieur* [It's nice to see you again, sir]," he says softly, extending a limp hand and swiftly turning away to polish glasses, perhaps afraid of further talk. The young woman I recognize on the Rue Catinat, once an assistant to a Japanese colleague, is bolder. She proposes a later rendezvous to pass me a letter to smuggle out to her brother, a refugee in Dallas. I suggest that a meeting might endanger her. She persists—then agrees and walks away sadly, the skirt of her gossamer *ao dai* floating behind her. One evening I visit a distinguished lady, formerly a dissident member of the parliament, and the interlude is hallucinatory. As I approach her splendid house, shrouded by a tangle of tropical vegetation, she sits at a piano on the veranda, playing a Mozart sonata. Her husband, also an old foe of the conquered Saigon government, has just been released from prison but must continue to attend seminars in Marxist doctrine to "remold" his bourgeois mentality. She regrets her past opposition to the former regime, explaining that "with all its faults it was preferable to communism." I try to stress the brighter side, noting that the "bloodbath" forecast by many Americans and South Vietnamese prophets never happened. "So instead of dying quickly," she answers, "we are dying slowly."

I would have hesitated to generalize from such a narrow sampling had not my impression of the gloom and despair been confirmed by even Communist sources. One of them was Nguyen Phung Nam, the official chief of press relations for Ho Chi Minh City and a frequent companion during my sojourn there. A chubby, amiable fellow who chain-smoked my cigarettes, he was a Vietcong veteran whose experience as a guerrilla dated back to the war against the French. One afternoon, over apéritifs, he casually disclosed an astounding personal detail. His wife and three daughters lived near Los Angeles, having escaped from Vietnam among the hundreds of thousands of refugees who fled the country after its reunification under Communist control. "Open the doors," he added, "and everyone would leave overnight."

Dr. Duong Quynh Hoa was more outspoken. A chic woman in her fifties, she had been raised in an affluent southern family of *collaborateurs,* the Vietnamese who embraced French colonial rule in exchange for favors. Her father had taught at a French lycée in Saigon, a signal honor for a "native" of his generation. She herself, unusually liberated for a Vietnamese woman, went off to medical school in Paris, where she joined the French Communist party. In 1954, back in Saigon, she entered the resistance against South Vietnamese President Ngo Dinh Diem and his U.S. supporters, serving as a covert Vietnamese agent while she practiced medicine. She was afterward appointed deputy minister of health in the "provisional revolutionary government," the Vietcong's legalistic rival to the Saigon regime, hiding in the jungles and traveling abroad on propaganda missions. One evening in 1981, as we dined in the midst of the exquisite Chinese and Vietnamese porcelains adorning her comfortable villa, she poignantly confessed her disenchantment. "I've been a Communist all my life," she burst out passionately. "But now, for the first time, I have seen the realities of communism. It is failure—mismanagement, corruption, privilege, repression. My ideals are gone." She decried the northern Communists who now ran the south. She inveighed against their ignorance of local traits and conditions and their heavy-handed methods—citing as an example their attempt to impose collectivization on the peasants of the Mekong delta, whose desire to own property had inspired many of them to side with the Vietcong against the landed gentry of the area. In her view, the northerners resented the southerners for having prospered from the American presence during the war while they, true Communists, had borne the brunt of the struggle. My guide, Nguyen Phung Nam, shared Dr. Hoa's animosity toward northerners. And their attitude prompted me to wonder whether a better understanding of Vietnam's regional differences might have led the United States to explore a sophisticated diplomatic solution to the conflict—rather than to presume that the Communists were a monolithic force in the country.

Focusing on corruption, Dr. Hoa told me about administrators at her hospital who padded payrolls, took kickbacks from suppliers, and pilfered precious pharmaceuticals for resale on the black market. She also pointed to the wives of Communist generals, who regularly flew from Hanoi to Ho Chi Minh City aboard military aircraft to buy up antiques, jewelry, and other valuables from the remnant bourgeoisie, which has been surviving by selling off its possessions cheaply. The abuse of rank reminded me of my days in Saigon, when the wives of South Vietnamese generals amassed fortunes by speculating in real estate, gold, import licenses, and other such ventures. "Exactly," Dr. Hoa replied. "This is still very much a feudal society, whatever its ideological labels."

But it was clear as we sipped Italian coffee and French cognac after dinner that Dr. Hoa herself enjoyed special advantages—not to mention political immunity of some sort, since she had

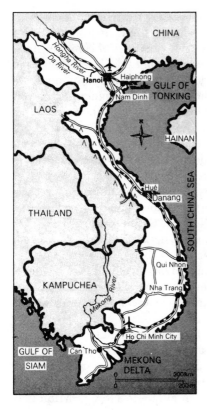

SOCIALIST REPUBLIC OF VIETNAM

Following South Vietnam's surrender on April 30, 1975, Hanoi became the capital of the reunified country and Saigon was renamed Ho Chi Minh City. In 1978 Vietnam invaded neighboring Cambodia, renamed Kampuchea in 1975 following the Khmer Rouge takeover.

criticized the regime to other foreigners. I figured that she could easily supplement her income by selling an occasional ceramic. As for her blunt talk, I could only guess that the authorities either abided her heresy in order to demonstrate their tolerance, or reckoned that silencing her might alienate her southern sympathizers—who included my press official, Nguyen Phung Nam. The morning after, when I cautiously avoided any comment about her, he volunteered his own opinion. Raising a thumb, he said: "*Elle est épatante.*" [She is splendid.]

One person whose sentiments I had looked forward to hearing

was Phan Xuan An, one of my oldest Vietnamese friends—or so I thought. We had met in Saigon 20 years before, when he represented Reuters, the British news service. Judicious and tireless, he had the best Vietnamese sources in town, and he had generously provided me with reliable information. Such was his skill, in fact, that my successors at *Time* hired him as a staff correspondent—the only Vietnamese journalist to attain full status in an American news organization. Knowing that he had stayed behind after Saigon fell in 1975, I had confidently expected to see him. But my requests for an appointment were repeatedly parried with vague excuses until, finally, I was told the truth.

He had been a clandestine Vietcong operative all along. Now, a top security official, he was off limits to foreigners. Hardly had I recovered from that amazing revelation than I learned that another old friend, Colonel Pham Ngoc Thao, a brilliant South Vietnamese officer, had secretly served the Vietcong as well. He had been murdered for entirely different motives during the war by Saigon government rivals, and his remains had been transferred to the "patriots' cemetery" near Ho Chi Minh City not long before my return there. If An and Thao had fooled correspondents like myself, they also duped the U.S. CIA, which had counted them among its contacts.

I was fed the party line by a senior member of the People's Committee, the Ho Chi Minh City administration, as we sat under a portrait of Ho in a reception chamber of the gingerbread Hôtel de Ville, the town hall, another splendid French colonial relic. A faceless functionary, he assured me that the "socialist transformation" of the south was proceeding apace as the regime, to popular acclaim, "fundamentally" eradicated prostitution, hooliganism, consumerism, and poisons left over from the dark ages of American capitalist influence. I thanked him profusely for the edifying lecture, which we both knew to be a formality.

The same evening, for example, three whores accosted me just outside my hotel with a ferocity unlike anything I had witnessed during the American era, when clients were plentiful. They could not have been more than 19 or 20, and they tugged at my sleeves with aggressive desperation, whispering obscenities in a mixture of pidgin English and fractured French perhaps picked up from their older sisters, or maybe even their mothers. Over coffee next morning, I related the incident to my guide, recalling the alderman's assertion that prostitution was being "fundamentally" eliminated. Nam frowned in mock disbelief. " 'Fundamentally'? Did he say 'fundamentally'? *Pas possible.* He must have meant 'theoretically.' "

The official Communist concession to sex, in modified form, is an improbable ritual—a Saturday night ball for "foreign friends" held in the former U.S. officers' club atop the Rex Hotel. The regime recruits the girls—office employees or shop assistants—and pays them a small fee to dance with Russian, French, Scandinavian and other Westerners, mostly technicians on aid projects. Colored lights beam around the elaborate room as a rock band blares and a singer, sinuous in her clinging gown, belts out the lyrics. The girls, dazzling creatures in stretch jeans and tight blouses, writhe and wriggle with all the verve of New York or London disco addicts. Then suddenly, at midnight, the party is over, and the Cinderellas go home alone—forbidden to fraternize until the next Saturday night. A European acquaintance, understandably smitten, pursued his lovely partner during the week, eventually luring her to a tryst in a secluded café. I indiscreetly prodded him for details later. "We just talked," he said with a sigh.

The puritanical curb strikes me as sound. For a poignant legacy of the French and subsequent American interventions in Vietnam is the unwanted children. The "Amerasian" kids fathered by U.S. troops may number as many as 50,000, the majority concentrated in Ho Chi Minh City and other towns where GIs congregated. Showcase orphanages care for a handful, but the xenophobic Vietnamese shun most as outcasts, denying them education, jobs, and even food rations. Those I saw—some with blond hair and blue eyes, others partly black—were peddling or begging on street corners. The mothers, many ostracized by their families, implore international refugee agency officials to

An Amerasian child selling cigarettes in Ho Chi Minh City

locate the fathers—often identifying them simply as Joe or Bill or Mac, to whom they were "married" for six or eight months in Saigon or Danang 14 or 15 years ago.

The Communist regime was initially reluctant to release the Amerasian children, calculating that they might serve as chips in diplomatic bargaining with the United States. President Reagan and the Congress were equally slow to revise the U.S. immigration law. But finally it was amended in 1982 to permit a few thousand children to join their fathers in America. Thousands more—neglected in Vietnam and barred from the United States—are doomed.

I have seen socialist principles transgressed by capitalist practice in Moscow, Warsaw, East Berlin, and other Communist cities, but never so flagrantly as in Ho Chi Minh City, where the commercial vitality of the American years still pulsates. Its avenues and alleys teem with stalls offering everything from American cigarettes and Scotch whiskey to French perfume,

German cameras, Japanese radios, and a cornucopia of other products, just as in the bad old days. Vietnamese living overseas send the merchandise to their relatives in Ho Chi Minh City; it arrives legally aboard a weekly Air France flight from Paris. Under the regulations, only the recipients are supposed to consume the merchandise. But they sell it to intermediaries, with the Communist apparatus participating in the business. Nguyen Phung Nam, whose wife in California ships him a monthly parcel, candidly disclosed to me that he could not make ends meet without trafficking in its contents. He also exchanged my dollars at the black market rate, presumably taking a commission.

The Vietnamese currency, the dong, is so debased that its black market rate oscillates between 10 and 15 times the official rate. Thus, as in Europe after World War II, the value of imported aspirin, vitamins, toothpaste, and especially cigarettes has escalated astronomically in terms of purchasing power—the spiral dramatizing the pressure of demand on supply in a land with a worthless currency. The arithmetic is startling.

A Vietnamese schoolteacher earns 200 dong a month. A pack of American cigarettes fetches 100 dong at a street stall. So, if his sister in Chicago remembers him with a monthly carton of Marlboros, he can quintuple his income. He can afford to buy meat and vegetables on the free market, which is furnished by peasants who are increasingly entering the consumer circuit. He can also pay off the Communist bureaucracy, thereby ensuring himself against harassment, or he can get involved in one or another of several lucrative rackets, like the exit visa scam.

The scheme is based on a regulation that entitles Vietnamese who have been granted exit visas to procure dollars at the fictitiously low official rate of exchange—even though they lack permits for admission to another country and do not intend to leave Vietnam. By prearrangement, the person issued an exit visa kicks back a portion of the dollars to the official who has authorized the departure document. The cheap greenbacks may be traded on the black market for a huge profit, or used to bribe other officials to hand out travel papers to relatives who can then engage in the same machinations. Some of the hard currency is usually converted into gold, to be laid away for future contingencies. Thousands of Vietnamese are involved in these maneuvers. And behind the scenes are the Chinese of Cholon—the mysterious Chinatown of Ho Chi Minh City. Like the Jews of medieval Europe, they are maligned and persecuted but continue to manipulate gold and money rates. The government relies on them as well for a range of other services, from transacting import deals to supplying scarce spare parts for vehicles.

Only a small fraction of the population has a chance to share in this heady action. Plainly, though, Vietnam increasingly displays that familiar symptom of Communist societies, a "new class" of entrenched bureaucrats and their favorites. The phenomenon is particularly apparent in the emergence of a *jeunesse dorée* [golden youth]—young Vietnamese who zip around Ho Chi Minh City on motor scooters fueled by black market gasoline and hang out in cafés that feature pop tunes played on Japanese stereos. A song that I heard frequently during my stay, recorded by a Caribbean combo, evidently owed its popularity to its melancholy lyrics:

> *I see a boat on a river, it's sailing away,*
> *Down to the ocean, where to I can't say.*

Both official U.S. communiqués and press reports asserted during the war that North Vietnam was being blown to smithereens by American air strikes. Visiting the region for the first time, therefore, I expected to observe ruins everywhere. But Hanoi and Haiphong are almost completely unscathed, and the surrounding countryside appears to have been barely touched. I was reminded of General Curtis LeMay's bloodcurdling cry to "bomb them back to the Stone Age." As I looked at the area, the thought crossed my mind that the north had not advanced far since the Stone Age.

If Ho Chi Minh City is sad, Hanoi is miserable. Apart from the mausoleum containing the embalmed body of Ho Chi

Minh—a facsimile of Lenin's tomb in Moscow—nothing new has been constructed there for 50 years. Nor is much done to maintain the buildings that stand. Handsome French colonial villas have slid into decrepitude, their windows broken and their walls mildewed. I was luckily housed at the Thong Nhat, or Reunification, once the elegant Metropole, the best hotel in town. Paint flakes from its ceilings; its plumbing fixtures, which bear the proud emblem of the eminent French firm of Jacob Delafonte, are cracked and leaking. Nobody notices when a rat scurries across the floor of the gloomy lobby, where superannuated European leftists and assorted Asian, African, and Latin American insurgents linger over drinks, still conversing in revolutionary jargon. Some are being trained in Hanoi, a certified center of the struggle against imperialism.

A few peasants, who have drifted into the city with nowhere to sleep, huddle on dark sidewalks at night. An occasional beggar is visible but prostitutes are not—though accommodations could be made, a Western diplomat informed me. Bicycles, the main mode of transportation, throng the streets throughout the day. Explaining the heavy traffic, my guide suggested that many people devote hours to the elementary mechanics of survival, going from one place to another to locate a piece to repair a chair, or to negotiate a couple of ounces of meat for dinner. The young foreign ministry employee also confided to me that he was usually so hungry after work that he spent the equivalent of his daily wage on an afternoon snack—an expense he could afford because he lived with his family. He woefully confessed, however, that he would have to marry soon because he was crowded into a couple of rooms with his mother and two sisters. Marriage was the only way he could find the privacy to be alone with his girl friend.

The northern Vietnamese seem to be remarkably cheerful despite their grim poverty—perhaps because they are disciplined after a generation under communism, and maybe because they never knew the affluence experienced by their southern compatriots during the American era. In an ironic twist, however, the capitalistic propensities that the Communists were supposed to obliterate in the south are instead creeping northward with alarming speed. During my sojourn in Hanoi, the party newspaper *Nhan Dan* published several editorials warning that the "neocolonialist culture" of the south was "expanding to the north," where it threatened to "spoil our younger generation and wreck our revolution."

The Communists cannot easily stop the trend, having been compelled by the economic crisis to loosen up in order to spur production. Like southern peasants, those in the north have been encouraged to sell their surplus meat and vegetables at free markets, and their earnings are giving them a consumer mentality. Private entrepreneurs are meanwhile emerging in Hanoi, though more cautiously than in Ho Chi Minh City. I dined frequently at a little bistro known only as "the French restaurant," concealed in a squalid alley. The proprietor, a former professor of mathematics, serves such superb *spécialités de la maison* as *soupe aux crabes* and *pigeon aux champignons,* accompanied by quite respectable French and Bulgarian wines. The place is not only tolerated by the Communist authorities, but patronized by senior political and military figures who spend as much on a single meal as they officially make in a month. One evening, the clients included a prominent Vietnamese general who paid his bill in dollars.

An obligatory journey for foreign visitors takes one to the shabby town of Langson, on the mountainous frontier with China, which the Chinese partly destroyed in February 1979 in retaliation for Vietnam's invasion of Cambodia. The Vietnamese preserve the ruins as evidence of aggression by their neighbors to the north, and distant rumbles of artillery testify to the continued tension. But for me, as an American, the trip to the remote site was significant for another reason. It underlined the ignorance behind the policy that involved the United States in the Vietnam war.

5

The War Nobody Won

The U.S. commitment to Vietnam, which began as far back as 1950 with President Truman's decision to help the French to retain their hold over Indochina, was designed to prevent Chinese Communist expansion into Southeast Asia. And it was founded on the notion that Ho Chi Minh was a pawn of the Chinese. But Vietnam and China have been enemies for 2,000 years, and their traditional conflict could have been exploited. Instead, American intervention in Vietnam united them in a marriage of convenience that fell apart only after President Nixon and the Chinese engineered a reconciliation that left the Vietnamese out in the cold.

Differences were apparent as early as the Geneva Conference of 1954, when the Chinese pushed the Vietnamese Communists to concede to a partition of Vietnam. For years afterward, hoping that a protracted war would drain the United States, the Chinese pressed the North Vietnamese to keep fighting—and, I gathered in Hanoi, actually reduced aid to them after they began diplomatic talks with the United States in Paris in 1968. The Chinese also tried to restrain North Vietnamese plans to conquer South Vietnam following the final withdrawal of U.S. combat forces

By MacNelly in the *Richmond News Leader*, 1973

from South Vietnam in early 1973. Mao Zedong deemed the prospects for Vietnam's reunification to be as implausible as his own dream of capturing the island of Taiwan. At a meeting in Beijing, he told Pham Van Dong: "I don't have a broom long enough to reach Taiwan, and you don't have a broom long enough to reach Saigon."

So America's attempt to "contain" China by checking the North Vietnamese was misguided. The United States could have conceivably taken advantage of Vietnam's historic hostility toward the Chinese, or at least have explored that option—just as, during the late 1940s, Yugoslavia's resistance to Soviet domination was encouraged. Instead, American strategists, hoping to buttress France's position in Europe, casually rejected the possibility that Ho Chi Minh might not be a pliable Chinese tool.

The American crusade, propelled as it was by the "domino theory" and the naive assumption that the entire region would

Geneva Agreements

The agreements reached at the Geneva Conference (May to July, 1954) ended the French-Indochina war and France's 60-year domination over the area. Participants were Britain and the Soviet Union (as joint chairmen), France, the United States, the People's Republic of China, Cambodia, Laos, the French-sponsored state of (South) Vietnam and the Democratic Republic of (North) Vietnam.

With regard to Vietnam, two documents emerged. The first was an agreement on cessation of hostilities; it provided for (a) the country's partition into two zones along the 17th parallel pending reunification through general elections; (b) withdrawal of French troops from the North; (c) 300 days for Vietnamese to exercise the right to move North or South, as they chose; (d) a ban on increasing military material or personnel in either zone; (e) creation of an International Control Commission, composed of India (chairman), Canada and Poland, to supervise adherence. This document was signed by the two powers whose hostilities it ended: France and North Vietnam.

The second document, a Final Declaration, expressed approval of the terms of the first document and fixed July 1956 for the general elections. This document was signed by no one, but was verbally supported by all the conference participants except South Vietnam and the United States. The United States said that while it was not "prepared to join" in the declaration, it would "refrain from the threat or the use of force to disturb" the agreements reached and warned that it would view with grave concern "any renewal of aggression in violation" of them.

The agreements also established Laos and Cambodia as independent states, completing the exclusion of France from Indochina.

collapse to the Communists if they won in Vietnam, disregarded the complex nationalistic diversity of Southeast Asia. Two dominoes—Laos and Cambodia—have toppled since the war in Vietnam. Much of Laos, however, had been a virtual Vietnamese province for years, and Cambodia suffered almost unimaginable horrors—more because of the insane cruelty of its own Communist regime than as a consequence of Vietnamese ambitions.

The full dimensions of Cambodia's martyrdom will probably never be known or understood. Nevertheless, the evidence accumulated until now already makes the Nazi holocaust seem tame by comparison.

Prince Norodom Sihanouk, the shrewd, nimble, tireless ruler of Cambodia, adroitly maneuvered for years to prevent the conflict in Vietnam from engulfing his country—a serene land of placid people. He yielded to the presence of North Vietnamese and Vietcong sanctuaries in territories adjacent to Vietnam, while acquiescing to American air raids against those targets. But in March 1970, while traveling in Europe, he was overthrown, and his ouster furnished President Nixon with the pretext to send American and South Vietnamese troops into Cambodia in pursuit of the enemy, and the war swiftly spread. Sihanouk's recurrent nightmare, he once told me, was that Cambodia would someday become extinct as a nation, remembered only by the mute magnificence of the temples at Angkor Wat. That day was fast approaching.

Sihanouk's successor, the inept and ailing General Lon Nol, shrank into the relative safety of his capital, Phnompenh, relying on American aircraft to bomb the Vietnamese and growing Cambodian Communist forces tightening their hold over the devastated countryside. On April 17, 1975, Phnompenh fell to the Khmer Rouge, the Cambodian Communist insurgents, just as North Vietnamese and Vietcong battalions were sweeping south toward Saigon. In five years, an estimated half million Cambodians had been killed or wounded, most by American bombs. Worse was yet to come.

The Cambodian Communists, originally organized and

trained by their Vietnamese comrades, had begun to assert their autonomy during the early 1970s. Like most Cambodians, they distrusted the dynamic Vietnamese, who had repeatedly intruded into Cambodia over the centuries. They were also swayed by Chinese radicals, who preached Mao Zedong's concept of perpetual revolution. And they evolved their own doctrines. Their leader, Saloth Sar, the son of a minor Cambodian official, had gone to Paris to study. There he picked up the undigested notion of an agrarian utopia, to be created by mobilizing the peasants—a reverie of the kind that Lenin had scorned as "infantile leftism." Returning home to adopt a mellifluous but meaningless *nom de guerre*, Pol Pot, he gained command of the Communist movement, and it grew rapidly after the U.S. and South Vietnamese incursions turned Cambodia into a battlefield. Then, triumphant in 1975, he transformed his ideas into reality.

At first, as they emptied Phnompenh and other towns, Pol Pot's legions seemed to be evacuating the refugees who had swollen the cities during the war in order to ease the economic pressure. But reports trickling out of Cambodia soon revealed a diabolically different story, which was confirmed later by the discovery of mass graves, piles of skeletons, and meticulous records, as well as the testimony of survivors.

The Communists were engaged in exterminating as many as 2 million Cambodians—a quarter of the population. Most, herded into forced marches or slave labor projects, perished from famine, disease, mistreatment, or exhaustion, and the atrocities included instances of cannibalism. Thousands of middle-class citizens, branded as parasite intellectuals merely because they wore spectacles or spoke a foreign language, were systematically liquidated. Several schools and public buildings were converted into torture chambers, among them a Phnompenh lycée, Tuol Sleng, which was equipped with electric shock devices, water tubs, and other such instruments. There the deaths soared to an average of a hundred per day during the first half of 1977, husbands and wives slaughtered along with their children—the victims photographed before and after their murders. The Communists proclaimed the advent of their administration Year Zero, the start of a "new community" that would be cleansed of "all sorts of depraved cultures and social blemishes."

The Vietnamese, after driving into Cambodia in late 1978, halted the slaughter and set up a surrogate regime in Phnompenh. But they have never portrayed their invasion as a humanitarian venture designed to rescue the Cambodian people from almost certain genocide. Indeed, they privately admit, despite their knowledge of the holocaust, they refrained from acting. The real motive for the operation, they explain, was their concern that Pol Pot's forces, underwritten by China, intended to embark on a campaign to annex the Mekong delta and other parts of Vietnam that had formerly belonged to the Cambodian empire. "When we look at Cambodia," a Vietnamese official in Hanoi told me, "we see China, China, China."

Cambodia's future still appears to be dim. An army of 200,000 Vietnamese, outfitted and financed by the Soviet Union, is skirmishing with a disparate coalition of three Cambodian factions backed by China—with Prince Sihanouk peculiarly aligned to the Pol Pot group even though the Communists killed several members of his family. Peculiarly, too, the United States endorses Pol Pot's representation in the UN—partly to placate China and also to penalize Vietnam for its occupation of Cambodia with Soviet support.

Foreign powers have been penetrating Southeast Asia for centuries, searching for wealth or influence, or to counter the lusts of their rivals. No surge in history had a stronger impact on Southeast Asia than European intervention, which transmuted new ideas and new institutions in the crucible of ancient values and traditional customs. The collision of East and West stimulated Asians both to resist and to adapt, infusing them with the vitality to recover their identity and to shape fresh goals. The experience also stirred Vietnam—and sowed the seeds of a struggle that was to culminate in the inscription of nearly 58,000 American names on a granite memorial in Washington.

Talking It Over

A Note for Students and Discussion Groups

This issue of the HEADLINE SERIES, like its predecessors, is published for every serious reader, specialized or not, who takes an interest in the subject. Many of our readers will be in classrooms, seminars or community discussion groups. Particularly with them in mind, we present below some discussion questions—suggested as a starting point only—and references for further reading.

Discussion Questions

What events in American history and what attitudes of the American people might explain why the United States would assume the right or necessity to intervene in Vietnam? How did the Vietnam war affect these traditional attitudes?

What was the basis of the U.S. commitment to South Vietnam?

What is the domino theory? What influence did it have on the U.S. decision to intervene in Vietnam? Was the domino theory valid? What do events in Cambodia and Laos since the war tell us about the domino theory?

What was the impact of the war on U.S. military strength, according to the author? What was the impact on soldiers who fought the war? How would you contrast the impact on U.S. military capabilities—and on individual soldiers—with America's experience in World War II?

By definition a war that is not won—or one in which stated goals are not achieved—constitutes a defeat. What mistakes were made by the United States during the war which prevented victory? Was victory possible? Do you agree with former Secretary of Defense Clark Clifford who said, "Countries, like human beings, make mistakes. We made an honest mistake. I feel no sense of shame. Nor should the country feel any sense of shame"?

The author argues that America has suffered a "collective disenchantment, known as the Vietnam syndrome," since the war. Do you agree? If so, do you believe this syndrome continues to exist? What effect did or does this disenchantment have on U.S. foreign policy throughout the world?

The author states that the Vietnam experience is having a strong influence over the current policy debate about the proper role of the United States in Central America. What lessons, if any, does Vietnam provide for this debate?

Why does the author say "the war in Vietnam was a war nobody won—a struggle between victims . . . . a tragedy of epic dimensions"?

The author states that the war in Vietnam ended the dream of an "American century." Do you agree?

READING LIST

Butterfield, Fox, "The New Vietnam Scholarship." *The New York Times Magazine,* February 13, 1983. Vietnam sparks renewed interest a decade after the last American troops left Saigon.

Fishel, Wesley R., "Vietnam: Is Victory Possible?" HEADLINE SERIES No. 163, February 1964. Historical background and early appraisal of the war.

FitzGerald, Frances, *Fire in the Lake.* Boston, Little, Brown and Company, 1972. An award-winning book that attributes American failure in Vietnam to cultural myopia.

Herr, Michael, *Dispatches.* New York, Alfred Knopf, 1977. Compelling sketches of the Americans who fought the war.

Herring, George C., *America's Longest War.* New York, John Wiley & Sons, 1979. An overview of the war by a liberal antiwar critic.

"Honoring Vietnam Veterans—At Last." *Newsweek,* November 22, 1982. Includes an article by Editor-in-Chief William Broyles Jr., himself a Vietnam veteran, who recalls the war the nation wanted to forget.

Karnow, Stanley, *Vietnam: A History.* New York, The Viking Press, 1983.

Kissinger, Henry, *The White House Years.* Boston, Little, Brown and Company, 1979. An account of Kissinger's first four years (1969–73) as President Nixon's national security adviser.

Lake, Anthony, ed., *The Legacy of Vietnam.* New York, New York University Press for the Council on Foreign Relations, 1976. Experts assess various aspects of the Vietnam experience and its implications for U.S. foreign policy.

Marr, David G., *Vietnamese Anti-Colonialism.* Berkeley, University of California Press, 1971. A study of the origins of nationalism in Vietnam.

Oberdorfer, Don, *Tet!* New York, Doubleday and Company, 1971. An account of the war's biggest battle by a *Washington Post* correspondent.

Pauker, Guy J., Golay, Frank H., and Enloe, Cynthia H., *Diversity and Development in Southeast Asia: The Coming Decade.* 1980's Project/Council on Foreign Relations. New York, McGraw-Hill, 1977. Studies by three scholars give a broad perspective on Southeast Asia's problems and potentials.

Sheehan, Neil, and Kenworthy, E. W., eds., *The Pentagon Papers.* New York, Times Books, 1971. The secret diplomacy of the Vietnam war.

"Southeast Asia: ASEAN and its Communist Neighbors." *Great Decisions '83.* New York, Foreign Policy Association, 1983. Topic 6 of the annual publication by the Editors of the Foreign Policy Association reviews Indochina's relations with its neighbors; includes a useful bibliography.

Vietnam's Future Policies and Role in Southeast Asia. Prepared for the Committee on Foreign Relations, U.S. Senate, by the Foreign Affairs and National Defense Division, Congressional Research Service, Library of Congress, April 1982. Available free from the Committee on Foreign Relations. Analysis and exploration of options for U.S. policy toward Vietnam.

Wain, Barry, "The Indochina Refugee Crisis." *Foreign Affairs,* Fall 1979. The author advocates "bringing Vietnam in from the cold while trying to moderate its more extremist tendencies."

Westmoreland, William C., *A Soldier Reports.* New York, Dell Publishing, 1980. The memoirs of a general who played a major role in Vietnam.

Zasloff, Joseph J., and Brown, MacAlister, *Communist Indochina and U.S. Foreign Policy: Forging New Relations.* Boulder, Colo., Westview Press Inc., 1979. Examines key political and economic developments in Vietnam, Laos and Cambodia since 1975 and analyzes policy issues facing the United States in dealing with these states.

FOREIGN
POLICY
ASSOCIATION
1918

Since 1918, the Foreign Policy Association has worked to help Americans gain a better understanding of problems in U.S. foreign policy and to stimulate informed citizen discussion of, and participation in, world affairs.

The Association is independent and nonpartisan, has no affiliation with government and takes no position on questions under debate. Rather, it seeks to call attention to, and to clarify opposing views on, those foreign policy issues which government and people must resolve in democratic partnership.

FPA's publications, in addition to the year-round HEADLINE SERIES, *include the annual* Great Decisions, *a briefing and discussion guide on eight current foreign policy topics. Reports on the annual* Great Decisions *"Opinion Ballots" are a valued index to the foreign policy views of informed citizens. Both directly and through the media support they receive, FPA publications reach out to more students, libraries, citizens and community groups than any other world affairs educational service today.*

FPA provides an open world affairs meeting service to the New York and Washington communities. Throughout the year, FPA's podium, with the opportunity of audience discussion, is offered to leaders, experts and institutions concerned with, and taking varying positions on, current issues of U.S. foreign policy.

By such means, FPA seeks to achieve what Elihu Root emphasized in the early years of the Association's existence:

"The control of foreign relations by modern democracies creates a new and pressing demand for popular education in international affairs."